Yorkshire Terrier

Tiny but Tough

WITHDRAWN

by Margaret Fetty

Consultant: Robert Owen
Yorkshire Terrier Breeder and Exhibitor

BEARPORT
PUBLISHING

New York, New York

Credits

Cover and Title Page, © Eric Ilsselée; TOC, © Eric Isselée/Shutterstock; 4, Courtesy of William A. Wynne; 5, © AP Images/Vadim Ghirda; 6L, Courtesy of William A. Wynne; 6R, Courtesy of William A. Wynne; 7, Courtesy of William A. Wynne; 8, © Mary Evans Picture Library/Alamy; 10L, © The Bridgeman Art Library/Getty Images; 10R, Huddersfield Ben and Katie from Stonehenge's "Dogs of the British Isles" Third Edition 1878; 11, © Geoffrey Clements/Corbis; 12, © Daly & Newton/Getty Images; 13, © Pets By Paulette; 14, © Laszlo Balogh/Reuters/Landov; 15L, © Olivier Digoit/Alamy; 15R, © David Ward/Dorling Kindersley/Getty Images; 16, © Paul Broadbent/Alamy; 17, © Sam Bennett/Swift-Bennett Photography; 18, © Mary Bloom; 19L, © Bettmann/Corbis; 19R, © Janine Wiedel Photolibrary/Alamy; 20T, © Isabelle Francais/Pet Profiles; 20B, © Isabelle Francais/Pet Profiles; 21, © Pets By Paulette; 22T, © AP Images/Mary Altaffer; 22B, © Isabelle Francais/Pet Profiles; 23L, © Isabelle Francais/Pet Profiles; 23R, © Joe Raedle/Getty Images; 24, © Neal and Molly Jansen/Alamy; 25T, © AP Images/Las Cruces Sun-News/Norm Dettlaff; 25B, © David J. Green-animals/Alamy; 26, © Ashley Love/Splash News and Pictures/newscom.com; 27, Courtesy of Rick Caran/jillidog.com; 28, © Moyseeva Irina/Shutterstock; 29, © Dave King/Dorling Kindersley; 31, © wojciechpusz/Shutterstock; 32, © Michal Napartowicz/Shutterstock.

Publisher: Kenn Goin
Senior Editor: Lisa Wiseman
Creative Director: Spencer Brinker
Photo Researcher: Jennifer Bright
Design: Dawn Beard Creative

Library of Congress Cataloging-in-Publication Data

Fetty, Margaret.
  Yorkshire terrier : tiny but tough / by Margaret Fetty.
    p. cm. — (Little dogs rock)
  Includes bibliographical references and index.
  ISBN-13: 978-1-59716-748-2 (library binding)
  ISBN-10: 1-59716-748-7 (library binding)
  1. Yorkshire terrier—Juvenile literature. I. Title.

  SF429.Y6F48 2009
  636.76—dc22
                    2008037169

For more information, write to Bearport Publishing Company, Inc., 101 Fifth Avenue, Suite 6R, New York, New York 10003. Printed in the United States of America in North Mankato, Minnesota.

032010
020810CG

10 9 8 7 6 5 4 3 2

Contents

Working for the Army

In 1945, during World War II (1939–1945), the U.S. Army had captured Luzon, a Philippine island, from the Japanese. Now the soldiers needed a telephone system on the island to communicate with one another. To build one, a wire would have to be buried under an airplane runway—but digging a **trench** for the wire would take too long. They needed a quicker way to do it. Luckily, they had a soldier who might just help solve the problem—Smoky.

Smoky

Smoky was a four-pound (1.8-kg) Yorkshire terrier (YORK-sher TER-ee-ur). The army was counting on her to run through a narrow pipe, that already passed under the runway, with a string attached to her collar. The string would then be used later to pull the phone wire through the pipe.

A modern military dog in protective gear

Many dogs served in the **military** during World War II. They guarded camps, carried messages, sniffed for bombs, and warned soldiers when the enemy was close. Dogs are still an important part of the military today.

A Tiny War Hero

As Smoky stood in front of the pipe, warplanes roared above her. "Come, Smoky, come!" called her owner, Bill Wynne, from the other end of the pipe.

Smoky bravely scampered into the darkness, squeezing past piles of sand that had built up inside the pipe. Suddenly the string that was attached to her collar pulled tight. It was caught on something.

▲ **Smoky stands in front of the pipe that she had to pull the string through. Luckily, she was small. The pipe was only 8 inches (20.3 cm) wide.**

"Smoky! Stand, stay!" Wynne yelled anxiously. Smoky stopped right away. Quickly, some soldiers jiggled the string to free it.

Wynne called to Smoky again. The loyal little dog crept forward. Finally, she spotted Wynne. Yelping excitedly, Smoky raced out of the pipe dragging the string. Smoky was a war hero!

After the war, Smoky and Wynne went into show business. Smoky performed tricks 42 times on a live TV show, "*Castles in the Air*," and never did the same one twice.

Bred to Hunt

Smoky was brave to crawl through the dark pipe. Her actions were not unusual, though. Smoky's **ancestors** were **terriers** that lived in Scotland in the 1700s. These hunting dogs often followed small animals, such as rats and foxes, into **burrows**. They had to have great courage to fight and kill the trapped animals.

Skye terriers

▲ **Though no records exist, many people believe that Yorkshire terriers are related to the Clydesdale, Waterside, and Skye terriers. These dogs weighed between 6 and 20 pounds (2.7 to 9 kg).**

The long hair of the Clydesdale and Skye terriers protected them from the teeth and claws of the animals they hunted.

In the early 1800s, many Scottish families and their dogs moved to England to work in factories and coal mines. Some of them settled in Yorkshire County. They **bred** their dogs with the smaller terriers that lived there. The result was the broken-haired scotch terrier, a dog that weighed from 12 to 14 pounds (5.4 to 6.3 kg) and liked to hunt rats.

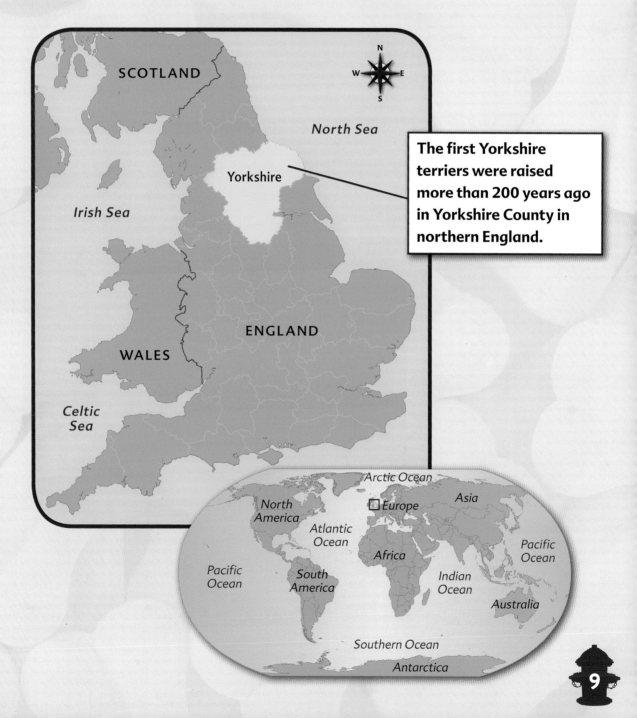

The first Yorkshire terriers were raised more than 200 years ago in Yorkshire County in northern England.

A New Breed

People continued to breed the broken-haired scotch terriers, trying to make them even better hunters. One of the best known of these dogs was Huddersfield Ben. Born in 1865, Ben was very **courageous**—becoming a champion at **rat-killing contests**. Ben was not only brave but he was beautiful as well. He had a long, glossy **coat** and won more than 70 prizes at dog shows.

▲ Huddersfield Ben participated in rat-killing contests just like the one shown here.

Sadly, in 1871, Huddersfield Ben (left) ▶ was run over and killed by a carriage. He was just six years old.

Soon others wanted terriers like Ben, but they wanted them even smaller. At the time, the size of the broken-haired scotch terrier varied. So people started to breed only the tiniest terriers, creating a new kind of very small dog—the Yorkshire terrier.

◀ **Rich women loved the little terriers. They would put bows in the dogs' hair and take them on carriage rides to show them off.**

In the late 1800s, broken-haired scotch terriers were renamed "Yorkshire terriers" in honor of the place in England where they lived.

The Yorkie Look

Yorkshire terriers, nicknamed Yorkies (YOR-keez), are just as popular now as they were in the 1800s. People still love the dogs for their tiny size and beautiful coats. Today, most Yorkies are about 6 to 10 inches (15 to 25 cm) tall at the shoulder. They weigh no more than 7 pounds (3.1 kg).

Yorkies with long coats often wear a **topknot** on their heads to keep the hair out of their eyes so they can see.

All Yorkies have beautiful, silky coats. The hair on their faces, chests, and feet is tan while the fur from the back of their necks to their tails is dark steel blue, which looks like dark gray. Some Yorkie owners cut the dog's hair short. Others leave it long and part it from the Yorkie's nose to the end of its tail. The long coat hangs straight to the floor.

◀ **To make a topknot, the hair above the eyebrows is pulled straight up and folded down. A rubber band holds it in place. A clip or bow is added for decoration.**

Yorkie owners often keep their dogs' ▶ **coats short because they are easier to clean. A short coat also allows a Yorkie to move around more freely.**

Tiny but Tough

Yorkies may be small, but they act like big, tough dogs. Their courageousness makes them excellent watchdogs. They will bark to warn their owners when they sense trouble. Sometimes Yorkies even forget how small they are and challenge big dogs.

▲ **Yorkies like to make friends with larger dogs, like this Great Dane.**

Yorkshire terriers are part of the **American Kennel Club**'s (AKC) **toy** dog group. This means they're one of the smallest dog breeds.

These intelligent dogs have lots of energy, too. They like to go for walks and enjoy plenty of playtime. Their curious nature often leads them into many adventures. For example, it's common for Yorkies to chase after insects and birds. Careful owners must keep an eye on their dogs when they're not on a leash so they don't get lost.

◀ **Yorkies are always ready to play.**

Yorkies are very curious and investigate anything that is not familiar.

True Athletes

Since Yorkies have so much energy, they make great athletes. Some of them take part in competitions such as **obedience trials**. During these tests, they follow directions such as "sit" and "stay." A judge watches and gives them points on how well they perform.

Other Yorkies participate in **agility** tests. In these events, they run as fast as they can over a path lined with tunnels, seesaws, and jumps.

A Yorkie jumps over a fence during an agility test.

Some owners take their Yorkies to obedience school, where they learn manners and how to follow directions. The dogs are rewarded with small treats to encourage good behavior. They get a certificate when they graduate.

Flyball is another fun sport that Yorkies enjoy. In this relay race, dogs jump over hurdles and step on boards that release tennis balls into the air. Each dog has to catch a ball and return it to its owner before the next dog starts.

▲ During a flyball competition, this Yorkie gets ready to jump over a hurdle while holding a ball in its mouth.

It's Show Time

With their beautiful coats and winning behavior, Yorkshire terriers often compete in dog shows. One of the most important events is the **Westminster Dog Show**. It celebrates some of the best-looking and most skilled dogs in the world.

During one part of the show, a judge looks at all the dogs in the same breed. The dog that's judged the best, according to the AKC rules, is the **Best of Breed** winner.

▲ **A Yorkie getting ready to be judged during the Westminster Dog Show**

Next, all the Best of Breed winners take part in the Best of Group competition. There are seven groups: Sporting, Hound, Working, Terrier, Toy, Non-Sporting, and Herding. The winner of each group goes on to compete for **Best in Show**—the highest award given at a dog show. In 1978, Yorkshire terrier fans were very excited. Cede Higgens became the first Yorkie ever to win this prize at the Westminster Dog Show.

▲ **Handler Marlene Lutousky with her champion Yorkie, Cede Higgens**

Yorkies that learn good manners can become **therapy dogs**. They visit hospitals and nursing homes to cheer up people. Their small size and sweet nature make them wonderful visitors for people who are feeling lonely or sad.

A Big Change

It's easy to recognize a Yorkshire terrier with its blue and tan coat. Yet identifying a Yorkie puppy is much harder. At birth, the tiny dogs have mostly short, black hair. They have spots of tan showing on their noses, feet, and eyebrows.

Yorkie puppies with their mother

Yorkie puppies are born with long tails. The tails are usually cut shorter, or docked, when the puppies are about one week old.

◀ **Six-week-old Yorkie puppies**

Yorkie puppies grow very quickly. By the time a pup is eight weeks old, its hair is wavy. Just a few months later, there is enough to gather into a topknot. Then at around seven months, a pup's black coat begins to change to blue. The coat will be mostly steel blue by the time the pup turns one year old.

A one-year-old Yorkie

Special Care

Adult Yorkshire terriers need special care to keep them safe and healthy. **Grooming** their coats is one of the most important responsibilities Yorkie owners have. The dog's hair is very fine, so it tangles easily and traps dirt. It must be brushed every day to stay clean.

▲ A Yorkie getting its long hair brushed

It's important for a ▶ Yorkie to get its teeth cleaned once a day to prevent dental problems.

Since Yorkies are so small, many young children often think that they're toys. They may try to pick them up by their hair. Rough handling will hurt the animals so owners need to keep a sharp eye on the dogs when they're around kids.

▲ **Walking a Yorkie on a leash helps keep it safe.**

Tiny Pinocchio is one of the smallest Yorkshire terriers in the United States. He weighs only one pound (.4 kg)! Tiny Pinocchio has appeared on several TV shows, including *Oprah* and *The Today Show*.

Great Companions

The tiny size of a Yorkie makes it a great pet, especially for people living in small houses or apartments. The dog does not need a big yard to play in. A walk around the block or chasing a ball in the house is enough exercise for this energetic little companion.

Yorkies love to play and have fun!

With good care, a Yorkie will live for 12 to 15 years.

Yorkshire terriers also make perfect pets for people with **allergies**. Many dog breeds shed their winter coats. This hair often makes people sneeze. Yorkies, however, never **shed**—not in winter or summer.

Yorkie owners often dress their pets in cute clothes.

Popular Pooches

According to the AKC, Yorkies are among the five most popular breeds of dog in the United States. Their beautiful coats, tiny size, and big personalities make them a favorite pet choice, especially among celebrities. Actress Paris Hilton often takes her Yorkie, Cinderella, to malls and restaurants. Even football great Brett Favre has a Yorkie whose name is Jazzmin.

Paris Hilton with her ▶ pet Yorkie (left) and Chihuahua (right)

Some Yorkies, like Jilli Dog, are stars themselves! Jilli has made many TV appearances. For example, she recently acted in an episode of the Disney TV show *Johnny and the Sprites*. In 2002, she appeared as Toto in the play *The Wizard of Oz*. Jilli has other talents, too. She plays cards and can shoot balls into a basket. Jilli proves that these tiny dogs aren't just pretty—they're tough and plenty smart, too!

▲ **Jilli is known as the world's only poker playing dog. She and her owner, Rick Caran, travel around the world to perform. Jilli volunteers as a therapy dog, too.**

Jilli wasn't always a star. Her owner, Rick Caran, first discovered the little dog on the street, hungry and abandoned. He took her home and fed and loved her.

Yorkshire Terriers at a Glance

Weight:	3–7 pounds (1.3–3 kg)
Height at Shoulder:	6–10 inches (15–25 cm)
Coat Hair:	Long and silky
Colors:	The fur on its face, feet, and chest is tan; the rest of its hair is dark steel blue.
Country of Origin:	England
Life Span:	12–15 years
Personality:	Smart, brave, curious, loving, devoted, energetic, good watchdog

Best in Show

What makes a great Yorkie? Every owner knows that his or her dog is special. Judges in dog shows, however, look very carefully at a Yorkshire terrier's appearance and behavior. Here are some of the things they look for:

hair on the head forms a topknot tied with a bow or the hair is parted and tied with two bows

Behavior: Should be energetic and alert

sparkling brown eyes with an intelligent expression

the line from the shoulder to the rump is level

very long face hair that is all tan; no blue hair is mixed in

legs are straight and end in rounded paws with black toenails

hair is silky, shiny, and hangs straight to the floor

Glossary

agility (uh-JIL-uh-tee) the ability to move quickly and easily

allergies (AL-er-jeez) a medical condition that causes someone to become sick after eating, touching, or breathing something that is harmless to most people, such as dog fur

American Kennel Club (uh-MER-i-kuhn KEN-uhl KLUHB) a national organization that is involved in many activities having to do with dogs, including collecting information about dog breeds and setting rules for dog shows

ancestors (AN-sess-turz) relatives who lived a long time ago

Best in Show (BEST IN SHOH) the top-rated dog in a dog show

Best of Breed (BEST UHV BREED) the top-rated dog in a specific breed

bred (BRED) mated dogs from specific breeds to produce young with certain characteristics

burrows (BUR-ohz) tunnels or holes in the ground where animals live

coat (KOHT) the fur on dogs or other animals

courageous (kuh-RAY-juhss) to be brave when facing danger

grooming (GROOM-ing) keeping an animal neat and clean

military (MIL-uh-ter-ee) having to do with soldiers and the armed forces

obedience trials (oh-BEE-dee-uns TRYE-uhlz) tests where dogs show how well they obey their owners

rat-killing contests (RAT-kil-ing KON-tests) popular events in the 1800s where a dog was put in a pit with up to 100 rats, and people would bet on how quickly the dog could kill them

shed (SHED) to lose something, such as fur

terriers (TER-ee-urz) any of several breeds of dog that were originally bred for hunting small animals that lived in burrows

therapy dogs (THER-uh-pee DAWGZ) dogs that visit places such as hospitals to cheer up people and make them feel more comfortable

topknot (TOP-not) hair or fur shaped into a ball on top of the head

toy (TOY) tiny, when relating to dogs

trench (TRENCH) a long, narrow hole

Westminster Dog Show (WEST-min-ster DAWG SHOH) the yearly dog show of the Westminster Kennel Club held in New York City

Bibliography

Donnelly, Kerry V. *Yorkshire Terriers.* Neptune City, NJ: TFH Publications, Inc. (1995).

Gordon, Joan B. *The Complete Yorkshire Terrier.* New York: Howell Books (1986).

Wynne, William A. *Yorkie Doodle Dandy.* Denver, CO: Top Dog Enterprises, LLC (2003).

Read More

Gray, Susan Heinrichs. *Yorkshire Terriers (Domestic Dogs).* Mankato, MN: The Child's World (2007).

Kallen, Stuart A. *Yorkshire Terriers.* Edina, MN: Checkerboard Books (1998).

Learn More Online

To learn more about Yorkshire terriers, visit
www.bearportpublishing.com/LittleDogsRock

Index

About the Author

Margaret Fetty lives in Austin, Texas, with her two miniature schnauzers, Cabo and Tristian. All three enjoy long runs in the park.